Leaving My Homeland

A Refugee's Journey from

Guatemala

Heather Hudak

Crabtree Publishing Company
www.crabtreebooks.com

Crabtree Publishing Company

www.crabtreebooks.com

Author: Heather Hudak

Editors: Sarah Eason, Harriet McGregor,
and Janine Deschenes

Proofreader and indexer: Wendy Scavuzzo

Editorial director: Kathy Middleton

Design: Jessica Moon

Cover design and additional artwork: Jessica Moon

Photo research: Rachel Blount

Production coordinator and
Prepress technician: Ken Wright

Print coordinator: Margaret Amy Salter

Consultants: Hawa Sabriye and HaEun Kim

Produced for Crabtree Publishing Company by Calcium Creative.

Publisher's Note: The story presented in this book is a fictional account
based on extensive research of real-life accounts by refugees, with the aim
of reflecting the true experience of refugee children and their families.

Photo Credits:

t=Top, tl=Top Left, b=Bottom

Shutterstock: Absent: p. 13t; Best-Backgrounds: pp. 22–23; Giuseppe
Carbone: p. 20; ChameleonsEye: p. 24; Javier Garcia: p. 7; h3x: p. 10t;
Charles Harkre: p. 12b; KittyVector: p. 6t; LagunaticPhoto: p. 12c;
Macrovector: p. 14t; Svetlana Maslova: p. 29b; Meunierd: p. 5, Seita:
p. 1, Olivier Tabary: p. 8t; Shawn Talbot: p. 25; What's My Name: p. 29tl;
UNHCR: © UNHCR/Mariana Echandi: p. 22; © UNHCR/Santiago
Escobar-Jaramillo: p. 14; © UNHCR/Diana Goldberg: p. 26; © UNHCR/
Tito Herrera: pp. 16–17b, 18–19, 27; © UNHCR/Betty Press: p. 8b, ©
UNHCR/R. Ramirez: p. 29; © UNHCR/A. Serrano: p. 4; © UNHCR/
Liba Taylor: p. 15; © UNHCR/Daniele Volpe: pp. 11, 16, 21; Wikimedia
Commons: Chensiyuan: p. 9; Murray Foubister: p. 10.

Cover: Shutterstock: Macrovector.

Library and Archives Canada Cataloguing in Publication

Hudak, Heather C., 1975-, author
    A refugee's journey from Guatemala / Heather Hudak.

(Leaving my homeland)
Includes index.
Issued in print and electronic formats.
ISBN 978-0-7787-3673-8 (hardcover).--
ISBN 978-0-7787-3679-0 (softcover).--ISBN 978-1-4271-1970-4 (HTML)

    1. Refugees--Guatemala--Juvenile literature. 2. Refugees--
Mexico--Juvenile literature. 3. Refugee children--Guatemala--
Juvenile literature. 4. Refugee children--Mexico--Juvenile literature.
5. Refugees--Social conditions--Juvenile literature. 6. Guatemala--
Social conditions--Juvenile literature. 7. Refugee camps--Mexico--
Juvenile literature. I. Title.

HV640.5.G9H83 2017   j305.9'06914097281   C2017-903577-0
                                              C2017-903578-9

Library of Congress Cataloging-in-Publication Data

CIP available at the Library of Congress

Crabtree Publishing Company

www.crabtreebooks.com   1-800-387-7650

Printed in Canada/092017/PB20170719

Published in Canada
Crabtree Publishing
616 Welland Ave.
St. Catharines, Ontario
L2M 5V6

Published in the United States
Crabtree Publishing
PMB 59051
350 Fifth Avenue, 59th Floor
New York, New York 10118

Published in the United Kingdom
Crabtree Publishing
Maritime House
Basin Road North, Hove
BN41 1WR

Published in Australia
Crabtree Publishing
3 Charles Street
Coburg North
VIC, 3058

What Is in This Book?

Leaving Guatemala

A **civil war** was fought in Guatemala from 1960 to 1996. The war was between the government and rebel fighters. Rebels are groups of people who fight against the government. The rebels were mostly **Indigenous** peoples from poor, rural areas. They wanted better treatment from the government.

Since the civil war, people have left Guatemala to escape violence.

UN Rights of the Child

Every child has rights. Rights are privileges and freedoms that are protected by law. **Refugees** have the right to special protection and help. The **United Nations (UN)** Convention on the Rights of the Child is a document that lists the rights that all children should have. Think about these rights as you read this book.

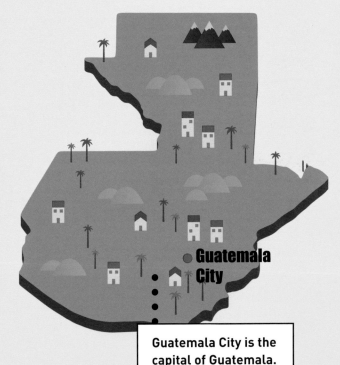

Guatemala City is the capital of Guatemala.

After the civil war, it was hard for many people to find jobs. The country did not have much money to spend on education. Many young people who did not have a good education and needed money joined gangs. Gangs are groups of people who commit crimes. Most Guatemalans feared the gangs.

Many former military and police officers were poorly paid. They started to work with crime groups to earn more money. They helped crimes take place rather than stopping them. People could not trust them.

Hundreds of thousands of people fled Guatemala to escape the violence. These people are refugees. Refugees flee their **homeland** because of unsafe conditions. Refugees are different from **immigrants**. Immigrants chose to leave to look for better opportunities in another country. Thousands of Guatemalans who were forced from their homes choose to remain in the country. They are **internally displaced persons (IDPs)**.

In Guatemala there are more than 250,000 internally displaced persons, including many children.

Guatemala's flag

My Homeland, Guatemala

The **Republic** of Guatemala is a small country in Central America. Four countries share a border with Guatemala. They are Mexico, Honduras, Belize, and El Salvador. The Pacific Ocean and the Gulf of Honduras also share a border with Guatemala. The country is known for its varied landscapes. It has many volcanoes, mountains, and beaches.

People first settled in Guatemala around 9000 B.C.E. Some of these first settlers were the ancestors of the Maya people.

Mexico

Belize

Guatemala

Guatemala City

Honduras

El Salvador

Nicaragua

Guatemala means "land of trees." It is a mountainous and tree-covered country.

Guatemala's Story in Numbers

There are two main cultural groups in Guatemala: Ladinos and Maya. Ladinos, also known as mestizos, are a mix of Spanish and Maya descent. Ladinos make up

60 percent

of the population.
Maya make up

40 percent

of the population.
There are also other Maya groups, such as the Mam, K'iche', Kaqchikel, and Q'eqchi'.

The Spanish took control of Guatemala in 1524. Guatemala was a Spanish **colony** for nearly 300 years. In 1821, Guatemala became independent from Spain and part of Mexico. Two years later, it joined with Honduras, Costa Rica, El Salvador, and Nicaragua to form the Federation of Central American States. Finally, in 1839, Guatemala became a republic.

Guatemala has more people than any other nation in Central America. More than 50 percent of the population lives in rural areas. Many people work in agriculture, or farming.

Farming is important in Guatemala. People there work hard to farm products such as sugar, coffee, bananas, and vegetables.

Martinez's Story: My Life Before the Gangs

I was born in a city called Quetzaltenango. I lived in a small, brick house with my mamá, abuela (grandmother), two older brothers, Carlos and Maynor, and younger sister Emely. My father died right after my sister was born. He was very sick.

Before the violence, Guatemalan children could safely spend time outdoors.

Soccer is a very popular sport with Guatemalan children.

Mamá raised us by herself. She worked very hard to make sure we had enough to eat and a place to live.

I was eight years old when we left our home. I remember our life there well. For breakfast, I ate beans and tortilla sauce with tamales (a type of wrap made of corn). Then, I went to school with my brothers and sister. I was lucky to go to school. Many children in my country cannot afford to go to school.

My school day ended at 2 p.m. I rode home in the school van. Mamá worked for 12 hours each day as a nurse. When she got home from work, I helped her walk our dog. Then, I did my chores until it was time for dinner around 7 p.m. After dinner, I played with my brothers and sister or watched TV, then went to bed.

Guatemala's Story in Numbers

In Guatemala, children start school when they are

7 years old.

School runs for 10 months each year, from January to October.

Around 150,000 people live in the city of Quetzaltenango.

The Conflict in Guatemala

Guatemala was ruled by very strict governments from 1821 to 1985. In 1960, a civil war broke out. Rebel fighters took a stand against the government. The government had been treating the Indigenous peoples badly. The rebels wanted all people to be treated fairly. The government and police forces fought back against the rebels. They also attacked anyone who spoke out against the government.

Hundreds of thousands of people were kidnapped, tortured, or killed. Some people disappeared. The government was responsible for most of those crimes. More than 80 percent of the people harmed during the war were Maya.

Cemeteries, such as this one in Nebaj, are filled with victims of the civil war.

Guatemala City is one of the most dangerous cities in the world. It is common to see police and armed forces on patrol.

The fighting lasted 36 years. After the war, most people lived in **poverty**. They did not have proper health care or education. But, they did have access to weapons from the war. Gangs began widespread drug selling, **human trafficking**, and robberies. These were illegal ways of making money. This also caused gang violence to quickly increase.

The country still struggles. It does not have enough money to pay its debts. Some government leaders, military, and police are dishonest. They help criminals so they can earn more money. The government still treats many people poorly. Many Guatemalans want to improve the lives of the people who are treated badly by the government.

UN Rights of the Child

You have the right to be protected from being hurt and mistreated, in body or mind.

Martinez's Story: My Life Is Changed Forever

One afternoon, I was doing homework in the bedroom. Suddenly, I heard Emely screaming. I ran as fast as I could to find her. She was sitting on the floor with my abuela. They both had tears running down their faces.

My oldest brother, Carlos, had a bad cut on his cheek. There was a lot of blood. He had been walking home from school with his friend Luis when a group of boys stopped them. The boys were part of a gang. They had already tried to force Carlos and Luis to join their gang. They had said no.

There are many reports of police taking part in crimes and treating people poorly in Guatemala.

In some parts of Guatemala, gangs control entire communities.

This time, the gang yelled at Carlos and Luis and threw stones at them. One of the stones hit Carlos. He started to run away. Luis tried running, too. The gang shot at them. Luis was hit by a bullet. Carlos was afraid. He kept running. He did not know if Luis was okay. We were all worried that he was dead.

I cried while Carlos told us the story. Luis was Carlos's best friend. I played with him and my brother after school sometimes. I could not believe Luis may be gone. What if Carlos had been killed? What would we do?

Mamá came home from work a few hours later. She was very angry and scared that we could be hurt by the gangs again.

Mamá was worried about our safety all the time. She had been thinking about leaving Guatemala for a while. Now she felt there was no choice. She made a promise to get us out of Guatemala as soon as she could. She wanted to keep us safe.

Nations Unite to Send Help

The UN is an organization that helps people in need and supports human rights. More than 190 countries around the world belong to the UN.

The UN has a department to help refugees. It is called the United Nations High Commissioner for Refugees (UNHCR). The UNHCR tries to protect as many Guatemalans as it can who want to leave the country. It tries to help them seek **asylum** in other countries. One way it does this is by providing shelters at border crossings.

The Children of Peace program provides safe spaces in Guatemala and Mexico for thousands of refugee children.

You have the right to special care and help if you cannot live with your parents.

More than 370,000 Guatemalan children are orphans. In some cases, their families have been forced to abandon them because they are too poor to care for them. More than 70 percent of Guatemalans live in poverty. Some children live on the streets. Others try to leave Guatemala on their own. It is very dangerous. Gangs try to kidnap or hurt them.

The UNHCR works with other programs to help protect orphans. They provide education to refugee and asylum-seeking children. They help children find safe passage to other countries.

In refugee shelters, Guatemalan refugee children receive proper meals each day.

More than 50 percent of the children in Guatemala do not have enough food to eat. Organizations, such as World Vision and Save the Children, promote children's rights in Guatemala. They give healthy meals to children. They also provide education and health care. But more help is needed.

Martinez's Story: Fleeing Quetzaltenango

Mamá needed thousands of dollars to pay a smuggler, or **coyote**, to help get us out of Guatemala. We were very lucky. Many people do not earn enough to save any money.

My abuela was a good weaver. She made scarves while we were at school. She sold them at the local market to make extra money. My brothers worked at a nearby farm when they were not in school. For months, we bought only what we needed to live. We were all scared of the gangs and knew we needed to leave as soon as we could. Finally, we had almost enough money. Mamá borrowed the rest from someone called a lender.

This sign in Ciudad Hidalgo, Mexico, says, "Welcome to the path of the coyote." The town is an entry point for coyotes who smuggle Guatemalans into Mexico.

Refugees travel many miles to cross at the border between Guatemala and Mexico, even from neighboring countries such as Honduras (see page 18).

16

Mamá did not know much about programs to help us in other countries. She just knew she had to get us to a safer place. The coyote took us to the Mexican border. First, we boarded a bus with some other families. Then, we took a fishing boat across a wide river. We had to swim the last part to shore. It was dark when we reached land. We had to cross the border on foot.

Mexico

Belize

Guatemala

Tapachula   Quetzaltenango

El Salvador

The long, mountainous route from Quetzaltenango to Tapachula is very dangerous.

My brothers and I helped carry my sister when she was too tired to walk. We helped my abuela over rocks and through ditches. We had to be very careful to watch out for traffickers and gangs along the way. They might try to kidnap or hurt us. It was very scary.

What Paths do Refugees Take?

Canada welcomed 2,766 refugees from the Northern Triangle between 2004 and 2013. Of them, 864 were from Guatemala.

The number of people leaving Guatemala, and its neighbors, El Salvador and Honduras, has increased in recent years. Together, these three countries are called the Northern Triangle.

In 2016, there were 8,781 applications for asylum in Mexico. Nearly 92 percent of them were from people fleeing the Northern Triangle.

Guatemalan refugees and asylum seekers often flee to countries that share a border with Guatemala. Many of these countries are small and poor. They do not have the resources, such as homes, schools, or health care, to care for the many refugees they receive.

Some Guatemalan refugees travel to Mexico through border towns like this one, El Ceibo, in the hope of one day being granted asylum in the United States.

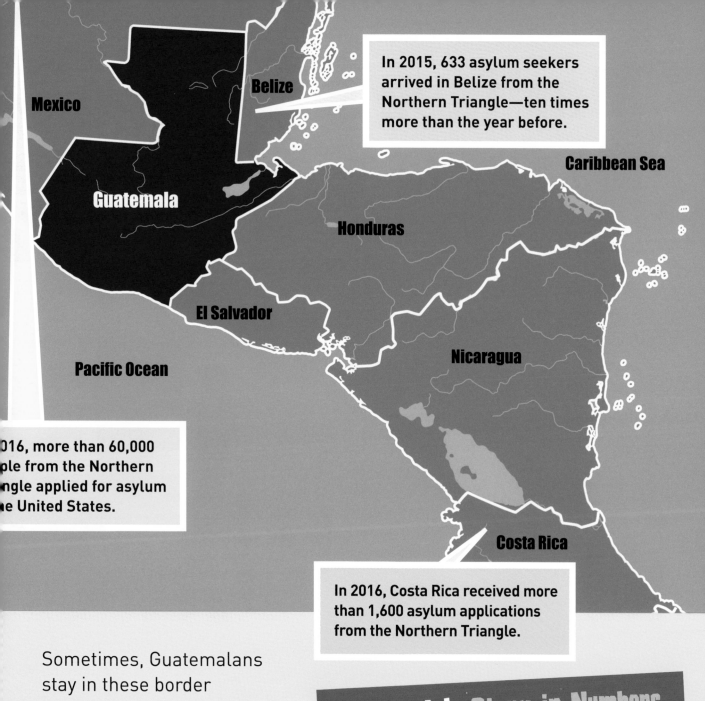

In 2015, 633 asylum seekers arrived in Belize from the Northern Triangle—ten times more than the year before.

Mexico

Belize

Guatemala

Caribbean Sea

Honduras

El Salvador

Pacific Ocean

Nicaragua

016, more than 60,000
ple from the Northern
ngle applied for asylum
e United States.

Costa Rica

In 2016, Costa Rica received more than 1,600 asylum applications from the Northern Triangle.

Sometimes, Guatemalans stay in these border countries. Other times, if they are able, they pass through on their way to countries such as Canada and the United States.

Guatemala's Story in Numbers

By the end of 2016, there were

164,000

refugees and asylum seekers from the Northern Triangle.

Martinez's Story: My Life in Tapachula

Our feet were cut and swollen and our clothes were filthy when we arrived in Mexico. Mamá signed papers with the UNHCR that said we were seeking asylum. We stayed in a **detention center** for a few days while our papers were processed. We wanted to be granted asylum and stay in Mexico legally.

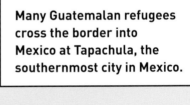

Many Guatemalan refugees cross the border into Mexico at Tapachula, the southernmost city in Mexico.

Then we moved to a shelter in Tapachula. It was very crowded and dirty. There was not much to do at Tapachula. I missed my friends. There were so many children and not enough people to help care for them all. There are gangs in Tapachula. But at least we had food to eat, and a bed where we could sleep.

UNHCR protection officers help make refugee children feel at home in the camps. They make sure the children know their rights.

One of the cooks at Tapachula made friends with my mamá. Her name was Yolanda. She was a refugee from Nicaragua. Yolanda married a Mexican man named Manuel. They had two children the same ages as me and my sister. We played together.

Yolanda offered my family a room in her apartment. It was small, but it was better than the shelter. My family stayed with Yolanda and Manuel for a few weeks. My mamá and brothers got jobs packing fruit. They worked long days for low pay. They worked illegally, but they did not want to cause any trouble.

UN Rights of the Child

All adults should do what is best for you. When adults make decisions, they should think about how their decisions will affect children.

Some Countries Welcome Refugees

In recent years, about 10 percent of the people from the Northern Triangle have left their homelands. Most hope to stay in Central America or the United States. Some have family and friends already living in these places. They are lucky, because these people can help refugees find jobs and homes.

In 2015, more than 230,000 Northern Triangle refugees and asylum seekers trying to enter the United States and Mexico were sent back to their homelands.

In Mexico, Guatemalan refugees settle in communities such as Maya Balam village.

In 2016, the government of Brazil set aside $1 million to bring 70 refugees to Brazil from shelters in Costa Rica and Mexico.

A program allows refugees from the Northern Triangle to bring their children to the United States. By August 2016, 9,500 applications had been filed, and 700 children had joined their parents.

In 2016, Australia agreed to accept Central American refugees from camps in Costa Rica. Australia plans to take nearly 19,000 refugees from around the world by 2019.

Not all Northern Triangle refugees are sent to live in countries near their homelands. Sometimes, they must travel across the world to find a safe place to live. Most refugees do not know anyone in these places. They must rely on themselves and the government to help them survive.

Martinez's Story: My New Home in Mexico

Many people left Tapachula after only a few days. They thought they would have better luck finding jobs and places to live without the help of the UNHCR. My family decided to wait. If we left, we would no longer be official asylum-seekers. This meant that if we got caught, we could be sent back to Guatemala. None of us wanted that to happen.

Finally, after 45 days, we got great news! We were granted asylum in Mexico. Only a small number of people gain asylum in Mexico. We were very, very lucky.

We were free to move to any place we wanted in the country. We went to Mexico City. Mamá got a job as a maid at a hotel. She makes just enough money to pay for a small apartment and our meals. My brothers work at a restaurant after school to make extra money.

Mexico City is the capital of Mexico. It has a population of nearly nine million people.

In Mexican schools, classes are taught in Spanish. Spanish is a second language for some of the Guatemalan refugees.

Carlos, Maynor, Emely, and I started school. The people here speak Spanish. We spoke a Mayan language called Mam at home. We had learned only a little Spanish at school in Guatemala. It is hard learning a new language, but I am getting better at it. My new friend Juan is helping me. We met on my first day of school. He shared his lunch with me. It was called chilaquiles. *It was made from fried tortilla chips mixed with cheese and salsa. It was so good. We eat together every day.*

Guatemala's Story in Numbers

Each year, as many as

400,000

people cross Mexico's southern border.
Only 1 percent of these people apply for asylum.

Challenges Refugees Face

Moving to a new country is challenging for refugees. Often people in the **host country** have a different **culture** than the refugees. They may speak a different language, wear different clothes, or eat different types of food. It can be hard for newcomers to adjust to these differences.

Guatemalan refugees may have the chance to become citizens of their host country.

Often, refugee children have to leave school in their home countries. It is often difficult for them to catch up on all the topics they have missed.

One of the biggest challenges refugees face is learning a new language in their host country. Many Guatemalans speak Mayan languages. When they arrive in Mexico, the United States, or other countries, they must learn Spanish or English. It is hard for refugees to fill out job applications and find work when they do not know the local language.

Sometimes, refugees are not able to use the services their host countries have for them. This may include health care, housing, or transportation. In some cases, refugees do not know about the services. Other times, they do not know who to ask for help using them.

Many refugees have lived in terrible conditions. It is hard for people in the host country to understand what the refugees have lived through. It can be stressful for refugees to adjust to their new life. They may experience **mental illness**, and need help. For example, people who have lived through violence may experience high amounts of stress and anxiety in the years after.

You Can Help!

There are many things you can do to help refugees from places such as Guatemala. Learning about another culture and putting yourself in a newcomer's position is a good place to start.

 Read books and watch movies about Guatemala. Share what you learn about the country and its culture with your friends and family.

 Write to government organizations asking them to provide aid to refugees from Guatemala. Together with your family, you can also make a donation to an organization that helps Guatemalan refugees.

 Be respectful of other cultures. Practice patience with people who are learning about your culture. Welcome **diversity** in your community.

 Introduce newcomers to your friends. At home or at school, invite them to play with you. Offer to help them with their homework.

 Ask newcomers to teach you some words in their language or to cook you a meal from their country. Do the same for them.

UN Rights of the Child

You have the right to food, clothing, a safe place to live, and to have your basic needs met.

Once they are safe in their host countries, refugee children have access to what they need to live healthy, happy lives.

Discussion Prompts

1. What events could you host in your community to help welcome newcomers?
2. What types of organizations help Guatemalan refugees?
3. Explain the difference between a refugee, an immigrant, and an IDP.
4. Why are people leaving Guatemala?

Glossary

asylum Protection given to refugees by a country

B.C.E. Before the Common Era; a time period more than 2,000 years ago

civil war A war between groups of people in the same country

colony An area or country that is under the control of a different country

coyote A person who smuggles Latin Americans across borders, typically for a high fee

culture The shared beliefs, values, customs, traditions, arts, and ways of a life of a particular group of people

detention center A place where people who have illegally entered a country are kept until the government decides where they should go

diversity Having a great deal of variety

homeland The country where someone was born or grew up

host country A country that offers to give refugees a home

human trafficking The illegal movement of people

immigrants People who leave one country to live in another

Indigenous Referring to people who have lived in, or are native to, a region for a long time

internally displaced persons (IDPs) People who are forced from their homes during a conflict, but remain in their country

mental illness Any range of illnesses or conditions that affect the brain, and therefore someone's emotional and psychological well-being

poverty The state of being very poor and having few belongings

refugees People who flee from their own country to another due to unsafe conditions

republic A state that has a leader elected by the people

United Nations (UN) An international organization that promotes peace between countries and helps refugees

Learning More

Books

Diaz, Alexandra. *The Only Road*. Simon & Schuster/Paula Wiseman Books, 2016.

Kalman, Bobbie, and Niki Walker. *Spotlight on Mexico*. Crabtree Publishing Company, 2008.

Knudsen, Shannon. *Guatemala* (Country Explorers). Lerner Classroom, 2011.

Shaw, Nancy. *Elena's Story*. Sleeping Bear Press, 2012.

Websites

www.countryreports.org/country/Guatemala.htm
This site tells you all about what it is like to live in and visit Guatemala.

http://easyscienceforkids.com/all-about-guatemala
Discover fascinating facts about Guatemala.

http://kids.nationalgeographic.com/explore/countries/ guatemala/#guatemala-volcano.jpg
Learn all about the history, landscape, people, and government of Guatemala.

www.unicef.org/rightsite/files/uncrcchilldfriendlylanguage.pdf
Explore all of the rights protected by the UN Convention on the Rights of the Child.

Index

About the Author

Heather C. Hudak has written hundreds of books for children and edited thousands more. She loves learning about new cultures, traveling the world, and spending time with her husband and many pets.